PLUVIOPHILE

Pluviophile

Yusuf Saadi

NIGHTWOOD EDITIONS

2020

Nightwood Editions
P.O. Box 1779
Gibsons, BC VON 1V0
Canada
www.nightwoodeditions.com

COVER DESIGN: Charlotte Gray
TYPOGRAPHY: Carleton Wilson

Canada Council   Conseil des Arts
for the Arts   du Canada

BRITISH COLUMBIA
ARTS COUNCIL

BRITISH
COLUMBIA

Nightwood Editions acknowledges the support of the Canada Council for the Arts, the
Government of Canada, and the Province of British Columbia through the BC Arts Council.

This book has been produced on 100% post-consumer recycled, ancient-forest-free paper,
processed chlorine-free and printed with vegetable-based dyes.

Printed and bound in Canada.

LIBRARY AND ARCHIVES CANADA CATALOGUING IN PUBLICATION

Title: Pluviophile / Yusuf Saadi.
Names: Saadi, Yusuf, 1990- author.
Description: Poems.
Identifiers: Canadiana (print) 20190201312 | Canadiana (ebook) 20190201320 |
ISBN 9780889713741 (softcover) | ISBN 9780889713758 (ebook)
Classification: LCC PS8637.A225 P58 2020 | DDC C811/.6—dc23

For mom 'n abu, suto api, apa moni, biya (and ibi)

CONTENTS

i.

ii.

iii.

i.

LOVE SONNET FOR LIGHT

I know a star in Andromeda broke
every colour in your heart. That you
shivered yourself to sleep in a meteor's
crevice or moon's crater whose dust
is now my skin. Beyond my finitude
you dream a wave and particle at once.
Know I love the way you warm my fingers,
pour gilt on my hardwood floors,
bear the universe's stories through bedroom
windows. I wish I could touch you—
not like two electrons repulsing, nor within
the semiotics of language, but hold you
how I hold a hand when I'm afraid—
and close my eyes when you're naked.

BREAKING FAST

The gestalt of my kitchen includes madness:
oval wooden cutting boards tinged with blood
and an electric juicer extracting the guts
from an orange. Terracotta flowerpots on windowsills
shelter exhausted purple hearts
that slump against the pane. The oven throbs.
On the tiled floor a fridge and pantry pose
as rook and bishop. Our ticking
toaster counts down the end of time.

My mom walks in and turns the radio on:
the adhan being recited to break fast. A man screams
or sings in cryptic Arabic muffled
by radio static. Steam rises
from haleem my mom stirs on the stove; the frying
pan's oil sizzles aloo pakoras. Seedless
dates on white china plates and glasses of water
on the kitchen table.

The smoke alarm shrieks its sharp
laments. My mom stands on a chair
and fans the alarm with a J-cloth—
as if waving a flag in surrender.

AMPERAGE

Why can't we harness sound for energy?
Skyline powered by Chopin, soliloquies
brew our morning coffee? I understand
the science, vibration/wattage, yet my hands
tremble to Shelley's chorus while I shiver
Arctic sounds. Diminuendo gathers
us to places without railings, of nearly trans-
cendental feelings, so how can children's
screams not turn an oven off? And we could
animate our cars with lovers' arguments,
a mother's non-stop babble jolt
a Macintosh, a faucet's dribble fly
a warplane. I would whisper *lay your
sleeping head my love* to flush the toilet.

UNPAID EDITORIAL INTERNSHIP

We stapled your promise
inside our eyelids; now we sleep
to your image in tapered blazer
and leather suitcase whispering,
If you work hard you can have this.
So we wake at seven. Cook lunch.
Daub makeup on irises, stuff
biceps with protein powder.
When the Visa bill arrives, lock it
in the mailbox until it growls so loud
we can't sleep. If there were a pill
for hope each pharmacy
would be sold out.

We patiently await our future.
In the meantime, skimp on TTC fare
when attendants aren't looking, barely
strong enough to push through turnstiles.
Add another lie to resumes under receipts
for arts degrees. Hungry until
we're nearly transparent. Bearing sisters'
hand-me-down dreams and inheriting
gas at a $1.30 per litre.

Sometimes we wish we could curl
(becoming as small as an Oxford comma)
into a warm pothole on a busy street,
live there as part of the city, regard
the world between total eclipses
cars cause as they drive by.

We've scoured wardrobes for soft cotton
fabrics to touch against faces like surrogate
mothers. Rubbed words together like flint
for a day's motivation. Alarm clocks
have towered above watered-down sleeps.
On rare occasions, we treat ourselves
to fancy cups of coffee, dark chocolate,
reveries. Writing poetry at night
with the rust from our lives.

I set up my apparatus on the wooden table: voice recorder, open
notebook, Sharpie pen and sharpened pencil. Across from me the
woman and her son sat on rickety chairs. I clicked the recorder on;
its light blinked beside the teacup that steamed between us. The
house's front door was half-open, sunlight wandering in shyly across
the floor over the mountain chert I had dragged in. From outside,
female Pashto voices I did not understand and children playing skif-
fle songs with metal debris and whistling folk tunes. I asked the son
if he attended school. He looked at the voice recorder's red light, its
cyclops eye, and inquired whether this was part of the interview. He
sat straight as if at a business meeting, his face clean-shaven except
two hairs above his lip that he must have missed with his razor. His
tensed forearms on the table were pale as mine. I told him to relax.
The aroma of basmati rice from the stove warmed the air and a fly
buzzed around our ears. I have to make sure I say the right thing,
he said. His English was immaculate. His mother pushed the tea-
cup toward me with thin, lightly wrinkled fingers, and shone a smile
that meant *drink*. I study literature in the university, the son said. I
came back to be with my family after it happened. He looked down.
I sipped the tea. Then I began the interview, and the son [His name's
Waheed. Maybe fit that in the article?] translated for his mother.
Our family moved into the mountains to be closer to God, she said.
I looked up to the stone ceiling and asked if she still felt God up here
after what had happened. She said, God was not in the sky, but in
here, and touched her chest. In the mountains it's quiet enough to
hear him. The daughter [I can't remember her name—maybe don't
mention her at all] brought me a plate of rice and placed it delicately
on the table beside the teacup. The son apologized for not having
any forks. I asked the mother what it felt like. The son, his back still
straight, continued to translate for his mother. She said it was like a

wind that makes people disappear, until sons and daughters are only names and words. She waved her hands as she talked. Sometimes the disappeared exist in the songs we sing. If they're fortunate, their names are printed in the newspaper where they live for a day, maybe two. But mostly they simply disappear. [Maybe, here, add reference to more commonly known disappeared people? Chileans under Pinochet?] I asked her if she ever thought of leaving, that perhaps God wasn't in the mountains as she suspected. She said, we cannot afford to disbelieve in God. We will pray for better lives. We will feed our children shrapnel. We will teach them to dance to the sound of bombs. The sunlight ventured further in the house, touching the mother's bare toes underneath the table. The other villagers told me many were burned alive, I said. What do you remember about the fire? The mother closed her eyes as her son translated my question. She said, Our families were carried to the sky in those heaps of black ash. They will come back down to visit us as mountain snow in the winter, and the snowflakes will melt in our palms [It's unclear here if the son poeticized the translation]. I sipped my tea. I turned the recorder off. The boy relaxed his shoulders and asked if it was over, asked if he could see the article when it was published. I told him I would try, though I didn't know how much space the newspaper would allot me.

PAINTING A FEBRUARY SKY

On this palette, will mixing *black* and *violet*
uncover the nameless colour
tipping over the horizon, grief entering
sky's consciousness, dark-plum wine
spilled and bleeding
from the other sides of the canvas?
My body lured to marvel
at its secondary colours, to trace
this page's primary words. When I mix
this much *love* with drops of *despair*,
do I create *heartbreak, inertia*?
Do I arrive at what I'm becoming? Words,
like colours, have gravity, they exert pull,
break in each other's wakes.
Isn't all matter subject to gravity?
Yes, but not like this. The way words pull you
into me, like *faith* stirred by *desire*.
To gather art to its primary source—search
for what has no name. Look up: *mystery,*
distance, beauty mix alchemically
to unveil this exact shade
of *moon*.

AUGUST, AFTER MOONSET

We counted shooting stars aloud
during the Perseids.

>   (I saw ones beyond your peripheral
>   and didn't tell you. I'm sorry,
>   but I needed them for me.)

GLOSSARY OF AIR

Air   Words are scarce
in our economy of .

Eyes   Your   resurface, gulp
the hospital's austere light, dive
back into body with your son
on the horizon..

Finish   We never   the library,
but each of us must decide
on a book to be buried with.

(Winds practising scales
above the deserted parking lot.)

Memories You share   made of air.
Flying into Montreal
penniless. Years later, worn
by physical labour, you nailed
an office job, bought a semi-
detached on Jane for 70k,
thinking of heir.

Never   I offer mangoes made of
air—ripe, golden.
From sentences you pluck them.

Perhaps language feels
unreal because we hold onto words
but   touch them—why
history's poems genuflect
to your single wrinkled finger,
knuckle crumpled like a page
I've fallen asleep on.

One   The IV's droplets pool mid-air,
fall one by   , tiny knocks
before God enters
the phenomenal world.

Stone   Your Bengali is made of air;
mine is broken. You perform
tayammum with a black   ,
unearthing your own father's
language into prayer.

SEMANA SANTA

Perched on a hawker's wrist the golden watches
tick in chronologic bliss (a block away a girl is late
for mass, turning stones to butterflies with a kneeling
kiss). She trails a monarch to the church—watches
from the door as her mother's crinkled fingers perch on
Jesús' knee, parched lips praying so earnestly in devotion.
She foresees the vision her mother will see once
the children are tucked in bed: a flock of gold
and silver watches flutter through the air, unfastened
wristbands flap beyond her blistered palms. She'll wake,
mouth thin as a minute hand, and utter psalms. The sun
will pour like sand through her bedroom window.
Juxtaposition to a slummy bar: a woman glugs a beer,
wipes mouth, leans in and slurs *Tomas, todos somos putas.*

READING BORGES ON THE MOON

Its darkened face is lucent. Craters laddered
and cliffs escalatored. Electric boardwalk to sublunar
oceans: a stroll in a light gravity.
You remembered *un bruñido disco* in your poetry
but your moon is not my moon. The one Plato
marvelled at when he respited from his nycto-
phobia. A burnt corona that blinded Homer
who couldn't spurn the beautiful. Or the madder
moon's omen in the sky after the battle of Badr.
Dreamtigers prowled among poachers of starlight.

In the future I find a field of deserted moonrock
and sit on a beach chair at dusk to read
Borges. Or to gaze at the Earth—a moon
to me now—scorched white from the old fires.

noise email news Netflix climate crisis marking groceries Internet
email news marking groceries *Toronto Star* savings finitude sleep
groceries student loans rest news Netflix marking finitude gro-
ceries savings sleep Internet email news credit card Netflix mark-
ing groceries savings love rest now email news credit card student
loans climate crisis marking groceries Internet email news car-
bon footprint family love phone finitude groceries Internet email
news pesticides loneliness Internet email news Netflix dreams
climate crisis marking groceries Internet email news Netflix fini-
tude marking groceries credit card *Toronto Star* savings grocer-
ies Internet email news Netflix marking groceries Netflix climate
crisis marking groceries Internet email news carbon footprint
family love phone climate crisis marking groceries Internet email
news Internet email news Netflix climate crisis Bangla mark-
ing groceries Internet email news carbon footprint family love
Toronto Star email **Yes it was cold outside,** groceries Internet
email news Netflix sleep **but I needed to walk** groceries savings
groceries Internet news **through the street** email credit
card guilt news Netflix marking **to clear my head** savings
groceries Internet email news Netflix marking groceries Inter-
net solitude email ethics climate crisis disappointment marking
groceries Internet email news Internet email news phone bill
Netflix climate crisis marking groceries Internet email imagina-
tion news family love phone bill rhythm dreams carbon footprint
savings Nietzsche sleep Internet email news creditcard Netflix
finitude marking groceries credit card *Toronto Star* savings gro-
ceries Internet email news Netflix marking groceries Netflix
climate crisis pesticides loneliness Internet email news Netflix
dreams climate crisis marking groceries solitude email ethics
loneliness climate crisis parents credit card rest imagination

AUBADE

for Nancy J

Hoarfrost eyes and myrrhed pillow.
Sky already paled. Blanket embering.
The sun's breath through your blinds,
oranging the minutes. You run
your fingers under milk-warm water.

        Sunrise crowned while I slept:
        blood on shivered clouds.
        Night rime crept through dearths
        of colour. Scraps of light.

NAKIR

You flew
from the city's peak with crucificial wings
and dreams of hiding in death's privacy.
The angels found you: their eyeteeth unearthed
your charnel, forced a gravestone in your mouth,
carved a question in your skin with bladed wings.
Who is your lord? You chewed the granite
until your teeth shattered but couldn't answer.
Soil constricted as your ribs cracked and bones
sang to skin in loneliness. Now you understand
the sudden deaths of raindrops—faces shattered
on eavestroughs without foresight to scream.
Now you understand how cavernous the mantle
feels for all the stranded bones that call for *home*.

FOR THE GIRL WHO DOESN'T BELIEVE IN TIME

I think of you the way two particles rhyme
across the universe, entangled but not in time.

Are experiences universal—love, beauty, exile,
particularities the simple garments of time?

You said a perception's not an experience,
only minor poets make love to time.

You told me everything is sacred.
Even prepositions luminesce in time.

You stand above your late mother's piano
observing notes crossing canyons of time.

Life's long enough to articulate one philo-
sophy with depth. What are we if not of time?

Just a boy, I only know the sun is given
to me, history a crude costume on time.

A glass of questions shatters on a laboratory
cloud when God drops a tiny vial of time.

POSTHUMAN

We were busy worshipping
words. Shipping worlds

through string. We held eardrums
to heartbeats to confirm

we were still alive. Someone unchained
the sun from its orbit. We watched it drift

like a curious child beyond the Oort cloud. Dimming
until it was another star in the night's freckles

and even the day lost its name. We looked
at our hands with unfamiliarity. Trying to understand

the opaqueness of texture. Our moulting bones
discarded. Our new elbows reptilian.

The latest language stripped of meter,
rhyme, beauty. We were warned: there are no straight lines in nature.

Women sang new myths. Men planted
numbers in the soil to see if the fruits

could solve our problems. We invented
new gods and crooned when we remembered

how to brush each other's hair. Music played
in a distant nerve. Insects danced

in a different hemisphere of our brain
or of the earth. We often tried to look up,

but we could only see our feet,
alien and hairless.

THE SPACE BETWEEN PAGES

I can only read after dark:
a nighthush snows on the city.
I uncage my imagination,
let it gorge on a trough of words.
The darkness scrabbles
at the window, at the door,
whimpering to be let in.
Safe in the security of words
until the page ends.

ii.

ROOT CANAL

Tie a string around my tooth and pull.
Offshore dental rigs won't drill this skull
for secrets. In my mother's tongue *I love*
you intimates *I want you as my home.*
In her kingdom, wand'ring minstrels croon
to cooling *kadams*, soothe bare gums with *paan.*

On St-Hubert a toothless snowman stares
into my window, smiles. This wintry air
is anaesthetic—ringing glass-on-glass
of interlocking crystals. Walking past
his porch I hear him sing in frozen key,
Novocaine would numb your face,
you'd never learn to love a place,
my abscess lulls to ancient melody.

PATHETIC FALLACY IN NOVEMBER

The moon's sallow rictus
on a November night. Bleary stars
barely keep their eyes open. The falling
snow invisible except under white-light
streetlamps where it rushes through
like TV static, dies mutely
in crystalline graves. The city's
collective sadness condenses
overhead
into brumous clouds,
migrating in aerial continents
from repressed regions of our minds.

Sombre in their sky march,
only occasionally looking down at the blinking
world, too proud to acknowledge
that if I held a clump of cloud in my hand
its heartbeat might understand
what November feels like
in its indecision that hovers
between snow and rain. Vacillating
degrees of frozen.

That if I dissect a cloud
    to regions
                deeper than
    its molecular love
  triangle, I will only find atoms
trying to fill silences between
      lives with stories.
  As if we are so different.

Remember: you are just water
and I am just skin.
Remember: despite their grace,
clouds are blind.
Forget: enchantment.
Snowflakes are your sacrifice,
signalling you saw me
look up before you had to drift away,
almost regretfully.

THE GOOD NEWS CHANNEL

for Matt

i.

Tonight on YouTube, cable and satellite,
a secret channel where clouds above
Sahelian droughts outlast your pessimism.
Moonlit rains beyond Tunisian plains craft
a jeweller's dream: in golden dunes diamond
briolettes carve diamond rivulets.

ii.

California redwoods bless the earth
tonight, invisible as gravity. Cities balance
on their limbs, our wars on their capacity
to breathe. They guard our beds tonight,
our thankless, private gods. A sapling roots
within the soil and gathers acolytes.

iii.

Tonight, there's no commercial pause.
A towhee by your window obeys the laws
of flight.

iv.

The laws of light illuminate New York
tonight—being shimmering with being.
The report tonight: poetry is news
that stays beautiful. Each word tunes
a tiny instrument for a clause's musical.
(In Gaza children dance tonight.
                    (But only for tonight.))

PHENOMENOLOGY OF NIGHT

i.

From cloudferries,
the angels
cast lines into the night
to reel prayers
from our human hearts—
      threads pulling
so desperately
           the clouds keel.

ii.

An angel unhooks
a worm of light,
heaves
an unripe orison
overboard to crawl
back inside us—
until it blooms
      with distress,
rises of its own
           sincerity.

SURAH

I'm intimate with three a.m.: outside my window
a garden rose glowers at her blemished
petals dreaming of bouquets. Potholes plot
assassinations of car tires, and street
lamps listen to all confessions. Shadows
cling to conspiracies of light. On the dead-end
street a solitary stop sign wishes it wasn't born
with a broken heart. A parking meter whispers
its prayer before bed: *In the name of God,*
most gracious, most merciful, thee do we worship
and thine aid do we seek…

The tungsten moon inhales its tidal breaths
to steel the firmament's architecture,
where a shooting star screams a valediction
as an orbit drags it to the sun; a white dwarf
recalls the warmth in the singularity's womb.
Young binary stars declare their love
and serenade beloveds with a prayer:
Will they wait till heaven shall come to them
in canopies of cloud, with angels rank on rank?

A stoic traffic signal blinks, and a hydrant
waits to prove its valour. Pebbles breed.
In forgotten alleys, discarded syringes hope
for resurrection while isosceles shards
from three broken beer bottles dream
of being puzzled whole again. They chant
a prayer: *In the name of God, most gracious,*

most merciful. Who holds all things in the heavens
and on the earth. Who holds the East
and the West: therefore whichever way you
turn there is our face.

The remnants of a party linger
in the tenements: a half-smoked
cigarette balanced on a balcony rail
dreams of the city on fire. An empty
bottle of spiced rum hums a lullaby
to which vermin droop their eyes.
Silverfish flit through slits in the caulk.
A spider knits a gossamer bed; its heartbeat
lures incautious creatures to sleep. A beetle
sharpens its pincers before a prayer:
If clouds approach wherein there is darkness
and lightning, they thrust their fingers
in their ears to blunt the thunder's peal.

In a musician's hallway a piano
and saxophone cuddle snoring
a harmonic scale. Jazz notes sleep too,
worked ragged in ragtime and
syncopation. An acoustic guitar
tunes its lower E string and strums
the meaning of life in A minor.
On the coffee table, a parched pen
dreams that poetry sutures sundered
hearts. It murmurs its sleepy prayer:
Thenceforth were your hearts hardened
into rock or harder still. For among

the rocks there are some from which rivers gush
forth; others there are when cleft asunder send forth
water; and others which sink in awe of God.

Air paints and repaints velvet coats
of midnight. Everywhere light flees itself
to nap, and all sound suicides in silence.
Even crickets pause their endless task
of sewing the world into song. The city
so quiet a grain of sand's heartbeat echoes
from a deserted playground. In my neighbour's
kitchen a grape starves itself into a raisin
and bananas curl in post-coital penumbra.
But it's almost four a.m.
My dream catcher mourns the hours
and whispers its final prayer before bed:
In the name of God, most gracious,
most merciful. Guide us on the moral path,
the path on whom thou hast bestowed
thy grace, whose portion is not wrath,
nor those who go astray.

CHILD SACRIFICE

The Inca believed black
    the colour of purity.
As I kill my bedroom
    lights, Juanita strikes
mountain ash
    in alpaca sandals—sips chicha
morada for warmth—
    and dawn gifts coca leaves
because the mountains are
    alive for you, girl with the noble
forehead, who will live
        among your satiated gods.

Dressed in your mamachumpi,
        two silver tupus across
your chest,
        and an airy cotton veil
that steels your face
    against the coming blow
to the head.
    A feather of blood
on the snowy
        vista, a violent death but
           feigning meaning—now a scarf
    swathes your skull, which stares
           east,
overlooking
    this world, its night not quite as pure
as the darkness before creation,
    stars so ripe you could pluck

42

them off the sky,
        stars like children floating on
a sea between countries,
        each breath a small eruption
of home. Do words
        in special order possess a power,
as in your people's prayer,
        or a poem?
I offer word on word in search
        of form while somewhere on that sea
a boy starves for a hand
        of rice
in his dying sky. God, please let his
        taintless spirit pass through all these runes
of my imagination. God, please, let his
        nameless spirit pass through all these ruins
of my imagination.
        And the girl on TV, corpse bloated
with brine, I lay her body in this line,
                        adorn her temple
        in layers
of gold—blood of the sun.
        Neck in layers
of silver—blood of the moon.
        Juanita, which words
                        will make me a good man?

TENZING NORGAY, EVEREST

Why

                the top of heaven

like walking

        ocean floor?

    Too much

             beauty

        this world.

Wind beckoning

you

to sing.

Don't open

your mouth:

this is the song

of death.

LOVE POEM FOR NUSAYBAH'S HIJAB

Cloudflesh gaped and skies above
Uhud revealed the moon's kneecap.
Survivors crawled among the dead,
eyes salivating. Your cotton hijab,
caught in windmoans, spelled a threnody
in Arabic while an angel towed the moon
across the sky. Behind you, mountains
flexed muscled limbs, shadows were pubic
patches. Yet no stare claimed your body.
Pupils slithered down your cotton veil, scrambling
for a form to fix you. Even I can't write
your hair, each tress a bridge to heaven's
door, although I gather fallen strands
which curl their English cursive.

MADE IN BANGLADESH

How to suck blood from this blood-sucked
image? A garment worker's needle is suturing
the scene: she sews a thousand polyester hearts
while her Singer croons, a schoolgirl breasts
the clock-less walls, Dhaka's illit-
erate mothers thread an English
logo, and a factory soldier stalks the aisles—
extendo lolling at his hip.

Nights ago, the garment worker drowned
her newborn in the toilet: half-submerged
in bloody water it groped the umbilical cord
like a rescue rope. The mother snipped the line
with fabric scissors. She stood on a red mirror,
whispered *all survival poems are washed in blood.*

EVE INVENTING POETRY BY HER WINDOW
DURING THE FIRST RAINFALL

i.

there are whispers in the letters.
secrets in their colubrine forms.
a raindrop streaks down glass *like*
my tongue down your skin. clouds
crumble and lick the window drop
by drop. sun-clenched eyes.

ii.

fingers, wrists, lips bursting
with time. we'll need a lifetime
for the clouds. a lifetime for stars.
a lifetime for the blind guitarist
beside the subway stairs, still
strumming songs about the rain.

ENDGAME

I'll rent a basement without Wi-Fi or windows
where my typewriter's keys evoke the nights
our rain was still gentle. And we'll have a black cat
named Samuel Bucket. One night, you scream *Fuck it*
and reconnect the Ethernet to scour the hookup-lands
in which I found you. In response I recount yesterday's
rumours (kids saying Lima was prey to another monster
storm). The death toll, charities, they're prolly making
rounds now on CBC, CNN, BBC— and God knows
the death or missing tolls tonight in some other coastal
town. Instead, unplug, ignore the screams above our
bedroom without windows. Board my craft Calypso: let's
float on this flooded earth where Odysseus abandoned
you. Isn't that when history began, so many years ago?

MILE END

From Mount Royal the dead watch over the city:
perched on tombstones they hum vespers and chew
                                   on autumn leaves.

Down St-Denis the rush hour cortège
caravans past café patios where October
beer foams from pitchers; on St-Laurent sprawls
of vintage shops proffer fox fur, faded
denim jackets, military boots sans eyelets.
The dead thrift-hop and smell the souls
of sneakers or finger breast pockets of
corduroy blazers in search
of their old lives. They hunt in vinyl
record shops for songs they fell
in love to: Raymond Lévesque trances
and la gigue fiddle dances.
The construction crane in the distance,
a giant tonearm in the sky.

Hipsters—vibrant with colour—prowl
memory's fabric for discounted gems, pull stories
from hangers, a rattle of coins on glass counters
and they vanish on ten-speed bicycles. The dead
follow their old scarves wrapped around cyclists'
necks and are whisked along St-Viateur
and Clark, or sit on handlebars
and fill with great élan. At night, they walk
hand in hand with dead chéris on old tryst strolls.
Riding La Ronde's Ferris wheel in silence
and crossing bridges of reminiscence

to school mornings when they ironed sweaters
and wool cardigans, sewing back buttons
on reversible vests—a time before
their clothes were ironic
and it was cool to look poor as a poet.

Now the dead smile, and hitch a ride on the brim
of a hat or sleeve of a coat back to their graves.

SONNET BY A FORGOTTEN TWIX WRAPPER

Petalled and split, our foil innards reflect
the ants who excavate for final crumbs.
In nightmares we remember thumb and index
vice grips reeking Bud Light, sex
and subway poles. Conjoined sleepers shrouded
in the TV's halo: champing on the parted
biscuits, (lovey on their sugar rush), evolving
such efficient jaws. Do their impatient tongues
perceive our frigid factory floors, conveyor
belts, and pitch-black crates that crossed
the ocean? Did they taste the cocoa's dreams
between their lustred teeth? Now we soliloquize,
though prey to seagull beaks, and sunbathe on
the asphalt when the maelstroms grant us mercy.

RILKE'S HANDS

So soft, straight lines
melt into curves—
each road in your palm
bridges the distances
between us. The brink

from loneliness to solitude
trembles as you walk, bends
at your will. Your hands
are ripe, and words fall
like fruit from your fingers.

QUIETUDE

On autumn nights the city judges me:
т streetlamps stand sentinel and measure
the hour's intentions. While angels prey
on sidewalks—shadowplay
from insects who weave leminscates
in the halogens above. Soon crumpled
into sewers and burped as steam
in square-mouthed manhole covers.

I wish the city would remain still
as God before he whispered stars
into being and the first ray of light
shrieked its birthing pangs.

Tonight, an asthmatic wind tears bark
from birch trees. A telephone pole reveals
its crucifix. Gibbets step out from shadows.
A gavel's distant thunder delivers verdict:
the rain's pounding may wake the dead.

iii.

THE RAINDROPS AT HEAVEN'S GATES

Patiently, we wait outside the fabled gates
to burst through *heaven* between the arch
of its *h*. We are harbingers of petrichor—
angels of rhododendron, emerald field,
blinding lily. Haven't you heard the madman
say God is a pluviophile? We built
a mountainous flower whose fragrance fills
the sky, but will it fit inside a human word?
Is there room for monsoon ecstasy, runnels
on a slanted window? Nightcrawlers,
dragonflies? A village puddle siphons
night's soul into soil. What would
heaven be without the sound of rain?

HUNTING

As I slip out the first
    third of my life
        memories like monsoons

wash through my skull
    searching for marrow.
        I remember Saturday's

breakfast cartoons,
    alarm clock guillotines,
        a toy telescope for the moon.

My adult self hunts
    through my childhood
        for identity

as I fade from
    morning's promise
        to what's left of afternoon.

Soon my mother will die.
    Her disembodied guilt
        will tuck me into bed.

Her memories hidden
    in her house's pipes,
        worries scratched on wallpaper.

Minor griefs cocooning
    under restless blankets.
        Emerging with wings.

TORONTO, 680 NEWS

for Suto Api

Traffic is the new god.
We pray in our cubicles
and sacrifice time to the asphalt.
Outside the office window, the daily pilgrims
begin their exodus while construction crews claw
holes into hell's sky. An eighteen-wheeler eclipses
the horizon without shame or feeling.
And the Gardiner's electric billboards tempt
us with discounted Italian beaches and palm trees.
The radio prophesizes delays.
         We exist between dust blizzards and plagues
of homeless who swarm on main intersections
to pant at our windows. Tailpipes grow exhaustfume
beards while the radio plays Rihanna over and over and
over and over again. Drivers unlock imaginations from
glove compartments and remember their children's
gap-toothed smiles. Even the rotting lake glistens blue
under the paper-white clouds and manila-folder sun. In the
distance, three birds disappear into an ellipsis. A police siren
parts the sea of tires on clogged roadsrampsstreets.
The green traffic lights are nasty, short and brutish:
advanced turn signals fade from mirage to memory to myth.
In a Civic's dormant engine history stops marching: SUVS
and minivans line up to refill their half-tanks of blood.
Nozzles drip. Sidewalk winos mock our carceral homes
amongst smokers exhaling slate tusks and cyclists
meandering the streets with Abrahamic faith. Downtown
buildings tower like massive gravestones, and subways

ship low-income workers through catacombs to finally die in their Tim Hortons uniforms. Students whose very blood is coffee sleep on the Spadina streetcar. At the crowded stop the bloated bus doors sigh open—a driver's apology tattooed on his face. Old women stand in the aisles holding Costco bags; immigrants stand holding Walmart bags; all passengers carry bags full of tomorrow under their eyes. Now radios report a collision on the DVP southbound. Our imaginations catch fire: drivers close their eyelids and dream of a partner's exhausted kiss, perhaps a laptop and leather loveseat, or a frozen pizza that waits on

the other side.

JOLIETTE

At metro Joliette with my jolicoeur,
we walked to the depanneur,
discussed dasein while buying
a Perrier and a block of beurre.
Outside, minus twenty-three,
with windchill it's real fuckery,
your back pockets warm my fingertips,
your cherry ChapStick so summery.
Take me to the everglades,
a place where flowers never fade,
but pans inside your basement wait
to fry us scrambled eggs, real buttery.

Blue sunrise on my palms, a peignoir,
a neighbour grows peonies in a baignoire,
I dreamt a homeless peintre
revealed Hochelag in a Renoir.
Make love inside these old maisons
until condos sail across the St-Laurent,
the vieux-accent is extinct,
and the cordonier's window plein noir.
Morning flurries, très légère,
someone's shovel scrapes fragile air,
a chasse-neige is herding cloud,
the hunched man salts his spiral stairs.

IF VAN GOGH WORSHIPPED THE MOON

Desperate for paint—as the moon's
starved white ribs through your louvred
window demand their sacrifice. You
disregard its signs until night's corvine
feathers begin to fall across your mind.
Or an autumn leaf, bistre and wine-red,
a rare beauty.

Alone with Theo's letters on nights so
long—each word stranded between pure
image and pure song. Starlight drips
across your pain. Moonlight walks
on water. And colours the only gods
to ever be: a saffron sunrise on
the sapphire sea.

PEDAGOGY

Ghosts at two a.m.: night unwraps its black sari
around your skin. I memorize each strand
of your hair, Jess. How high your soprano
peaks before it cracks; how long your laughter
squeaks until it dies. (Please don't close your eyes.
Or even blink. I'd deafen at a lash's avalanche.)
Let's teach the Greeks the constellations
of your jewellery, Jess. Measure tangents
in your palm lines; the Earth isn't flat
at the slopes of your shoulders.
Dawn wimples us. Rain dimples
the pond where you learned
to dream under-
water.

FORESHADOWS

after Nandalal Bose's "New Clouds"

Storm clouds will drag mahogany darkness into palm
forests, wispy mist over quilted rice fields.
Inside nimbi, monsoons will uncoil kilometre-long
chain-links before heaving them over icy bannisters.
A farmer drops his scythe, shouts a word whose meaning
winds scratch apart. A black mynah braves heart
attacks mid-air, and a girl sketches clouds on stone
floors in Viswa-Bharati—smudges their edges for aesthetic
effect, wonders if humans alone feel beauty, how pathetic
pathos is, if two field cows bellowing different pitches
mean music. A boy with an open umbrella will bicycle
by her door; paintbrushes revert to coconut trees.
Shortly, the first cloud will arrive lugging a factory
of shadows behind it; women haul basmati
husks across dirt paths, anklets chiming. The doyen
clutches her white sari hem, looks up at everything
that will be, asks the first cloud if beauty is invitation.

THE PLACE WORDS GO TO DIE

Primifluous was there and wandered murk-eyed
in the river's bones where sand is consanguineous
with hornfels, slag and stones whose names

unskin themselves. The pyres crackle in the night:
saxum sacrificed and born again as *saxifrage, carnem*
reincarnates as *carnation* whose silken petals

fumigate the flesh. So many old ones perished without
eulogy—no holy words for holy words that burned—
all dreamt of future human vessels to ferry them

through time. *Verily* steps toward the flame: thou shalt
be resurrected full of glory on marijuana-crusted lips
that puff puff pass and holler about going *viral*

on the strip, as megabytes on fibre optic wires,
in tongues that sip sangría to discuss the quarter's
profits (still the pyres tantrum through the night),

reborn as *chinkle* when we toast to better lives, as friday
nite's halfdrunkn txts to formr wifes, (*mors'*
renaissance as *immortality*), revivified as women's

moans in gaudy New York strip clubs, (*facudita*'s
afterlives as *fuck you, Foucault, fakir*), or born again
as rifle shots in Pakistan (bullets growing wings

until they're plovers in the sky aiming for the place
birds go to die). The stars abandoned us;
even clouds, once shipwrecked in the night,

are gone. And when the last bird sang, its final notes
foretold skies would splinter like cracked glass, jagged
shards would rain toward awaiting open mouths.

THE FLOWER MARKET

Kolkata, Present Day
My taxi driver's lost again,
still pitching brothels, booze,
a sunset river cruise. The cab
is weaving like it's in a movie,
but we're only driving through
a poem, and I'm only looking
for the flower market.

> *Flashback, Kolkata, 1943*
> The girl stabs the alley cat mid-meow,
> mother fries the meat with kerosene.
> It's WWII, bodies thin as letters.
> The boy is eating a rose's petals in
> the corner, his younger sister bites
> the stems. Then we move to a night
> no lens can follow—no cats wander,
> flowers don't perfume. Barely bones,
> the girl is lisping Tagore's poetry,
> trying to breathe the flowers
> in his lines, or inhale the letters
> that almost look in bloom: ণ প শ

Kolkata, Present Day
Still lost, the driver demands more fare.
He's a villain now, hair slicked back.
When I find the flower market, petals
await my zoom. The vendors smile,
broken teeth and all, sell me blood-
red garlands for twice the local price.

ROAD TRIP DICTIONARY

Aletheia: watching through the rear-view mirror as the sunset smelts the clouds, turning the sky to burned steel, while the darkening road pulls you east

Clouding: using once dead-time to admire the democratic beauty of the sky and realizing Luke Howard's clumsiness

God is dead: exclamatory remark used when Google Maps sends one in circles while trying to find a hole-in-the-wall

Rain croaks: hallucinating the windshield wipers' metronomic rhythm even while the sun is gorging on the sky

Scantion: uneven and often jagged cursive or print produced while attempting to write poetry in a speeding vehicle

Semogembee: the golden wheat fields gleaming through the open window which melt into a gilded pool as your eyes begin to water

Taking a baby: sleeping in fetal-position on the passenger's seat and remembering when you didn't know the way home once you were three blocks from the porch

Vastity: when the constellations crystallize and fade as you turn the radio dial

THE TAXI DRIVER'S THERAPY

for Swati

KOLKATA'S KLAXONS corrode the wiring in
your skull: a child, you watched the Brahmin
sacrifice a goat at Kali temple, bare feet were
islands on its blood. Your mother whispered
this is how we cleanse our hearts, but you can't
recall what *this* means. Now you're hanging
a bare foot from your taxi window, blistered
toes antennae to scan the city for her voice.
Instead of Ma's eyes, you dream of two black
crows sharing a cigarette on an awning—
they light another, alight together for
wherever crows go when outside of human
experience. Your side mirror sniffs at women's
silken saris; the writing on the mirror states
summer is a time for reveries. In the alley, people
are moving through each other, not ghosts,
but so alive their skins a porous border.

SPACETIME

We Twitter, Tinder, Tumblr through eternity. Loquacious
text messages flit from fingertips, waves of data spill
through our skulls. Every cm^2 of oxygen overflowing
with bank PINs, girls in yoga pants, the frequencies
of whale cries. Digital clouds brim with selfies and rain
videos on how to cook coconut shrimp. Sepia-filtered
photographs prowl for leaks in blood-brain barriers. Outside
our windows tree roots evolve into wires and birds trilling
sing the world electric. Every night we Facetime-kiss perfect
glass lips before bed and utter our sincerest prayers to our daily
blogs. We travel the world from screen to screen (breast
to breast incognito). The shortest distance between
home and work is a TV episode. Each hour is twenty songs.
We have lived a hundred lives in a breath and court ten lonely
women with a click. Emails trundle on invisible tracks of sky,
racing sexting winks and viral videos for our attention. Air
is composed of pixels and a radio bleeds white static. The world's
digital heartbeat only slows when I face the empty stare of a dead
battery. A boy on the subway scans my image without blinking.
Women download my face in a glance. A minute is tortured.
Lifetimes breed under each fingernail and wait to explode.

IS THE AFTERLIFE LONELY TOO?

Outside of Kantian space and time, do you miss dancing
in dusty basements where sex was once phenomenal?

How sunlight threads in morning frost, breath pluming
in knots between you and the snow-marbled fields?

When depression knocks, do the dead hide inside
poems, in the corridors between stanzas, curling fetal

in a b's womb? (Are you here, now?) When the dead speak,
do words signify perfectly with presence? Does each

sentence sound like a symphony? Or appear in the mind's
eye in 4k imagery? Have you ever walked across the surface

of a star? Are they as lonely as they look in my city sky?
Do you dream of microwaves beeping? Or reading Kafka

whose words are black scars? What do the dead think about
after the afterglow, if no one's breathing? Don't you miss

feeling, feeling, feeling? And failing, the soul search that
follows, from which you promise yourself to be reborn?

FLOWERS ON EUROPA

Autumn leaves don't crackle; skylarks
never sing; a touch of rainfall breaks
the bed. Do daffodils dissolve in your
unpractised inner eye? Each tulip spoor
clichéd, the orchids picked and roses dead.
Tonight I grow a darkness in my head.
Imagine frozen plumes above Europa:
the creaking ice is musical. The sun's iotas
feed extremophiles. And undiscovered flowers
flare within the doldrums. Glowing
petals shock the frost and sepals hug
themselves for warmth. The anthers drug
the moon with blanched light—imagined
from our window while we waste the night.

LULLABIES

i want to read a story with you—a glass
of red wine at bedtime, but tonight
murakami won't do.

turning pages warms my fingers, though your toes
are dots of ice. let's read a scene together—
juliet's balcony won't suffice.

tomorrow's already on your skin, and sleep invades
your eyes. i'll read a sonnet for you—
although tonight neruda lies.

i want to write a story with you—page and plot
are set. before you fall asleep tonight,
i'll mouth the alphabet.

BELITTLE

The word I learned when you confessed
your dad belittled your puny, puny heart
with fists smouldering through the night.
And *hence*—which you applied in essays
to reach conclusions—now writing
hence, having exhausted *thus, therefore,*
consequently, it reminds me of you.
Strange how we retain pieces of
language, the way Yeats holds *terrible*
for me, as in terrible beauty, or Rumi
beloved for you, as in beloved let me enter.

As you fade further in memory, I'll forget
your voice's timbre when you wept,
lose the scars above your nose (already
I've forgotten their shapes). Hence,
I'll only think of you on chance
encounters in novels, essays, poems—
in lines searching for conclusions.

PLEASURING SHAHRAZAD

In rosewater I rinse
my final words, dip
them into your body.
Your slow, saline drip
on my tongue. You eclipse
Medinan dates soaked
in honey, saffron rice
with diced pistachios,
a single pomegranate—
surah carved in Kufic
on each ruby seed.
Camphor recites its being
inside a kerosene lamp.

Don't plead, simply ask
for pleasure pleated
upon pleasure past
tongue-winding rinds
around words.
Damascus musk settles
on damask pillows.
Iced watermelon wine
gushes in crystal glass.
Hebron peaches blush;
sea-coast lemons
        cleave in halves.
My nails moonrake
damp thighs;
again, I dine on
webbed-wet fingers.

Lips graze lashes, kohl.
On each closed eyelid
my tongue practises
its patient whorl
before I cherish
your perfect pearl.
I gave my day
dreaming of your
myrrh's mystique.
Now my tongue
is to caress—
not to speak.

NOTES & ACKNOWLEDGEMENTS

Thank you to family—Mom 'n Abu, Suto Api, Apa Moni, Biya, Ibi— and friends, particularly old friends—Brito, Gurjit—but also all the people I've met more recently, especially Matt, Phil and Momo.

Thank you to all my teachers and mentors at York, UVic, and Banff who supported me, particularly Chris Gudgeon and Eric Miller.

Thank you to everyone at Nightwood, but especially Carleton and Silas who made the book much better.

Thanks to *The Malahat Review* where "The Place Words Go to Die," "Reading Borges on the Moon," "Joliette" and "Pleasuring Shahrazad" first appeared.

Thanks to *Vallum* and its chapbook series where "Pedagogy," "Sonnet for a Forgotten Twix Wrapper," "Amperage," "Love Poem for Nusaybah's Hijab," "Love Poem for Light," "Flowers on Europa," "Quietude," "Pathetic Fallacy in November," "Rilke's Hands," "Spacetime," "The Taxi Driver's Therapy," "Mild End" and "Is the Afterlife Lonely Too?" first appeared.

Thanks to *Hamilton Arts & Letters* where "eve inventing poetry by her window during the first rainfall" and "Belittle" first appeared.

Thanks to *Canadian Notes & Queries* where "Root Canal" first appeared.

Thanks to *untethered* where "Aubade" and "Posthuman" first appeared.

Thanks to *Brick Magazine* where "The Good News Channel" first appeared.

Thanks to *The Quilliad* where "Rough Draft," "August, After Moonset," and "noise" first appeared.

Thanks to *PRISM international* where "Breaking Fast" first appeared.

Thanks to *Contemporary Verse 2* where "Made in Bangladesh" first appeared.

Thanks to *Prairie Fire* where "Hunting" first appeared.

Thanks to *wildness* where "Painting a February Sky" first appeared.

Thanks to *This* where "Unpaid Editorial Internship" first appeared.

NOTE ON THE TITLE: "Pluviophile" is not coined by me, and it is used frequently elsewhere even though the suffix "phile" should go with a Greek compound and not the Latin "pluvio." I've grown partial to the word, even if (and partly because) it has been coined with an error in its heart.

ABOUT THE AUTHOR

Yusuf Saadi's writing has appeared in journals including *The Malahat Review*, *Vallum*, *Brick*, *Best Canadian Poetry 2019*, *Best Canadian Poetry 2018*, *Grain*, *CV2*, *Prairie Fire*, *PRISM international*, *Canadian Notes & Queries*, *Hamilton Arts & Letters*, *This* and *untethered*. He won the 2016 *Vallum* Chapbook Award and *The Malahat Review*'s 2016 Far Horizons Award for Poetry. He holds an MA in English from the University of Victoria.